Original cover art by
Alison Porras and Sarah Roderick

Dedicated to the men, women, and children whose lives,

Whether directly or indirectly,

Are negatively impacted by racism and social injustice.

CAST OF CHARACTERS

INTRODUCTION NARRATORS
MICHELLE OBAMA NARRATOR
JULIE
JAEL
TATI 1 - 4
CHRIS
DANA 1 & 2
DARIAN
JAIME
R.P.
MAY
KAYLA
JULIANNA
STEPHANIE
NADEGE
PAM
HERNZ
FREDDIE 1 - 10
ANDREW 1 - 4
JOE 1 - 3
KIARA 1 - 7
WHITE MALE FRIEND
THE GIRLFRIEND
STEVEN
LAURA
HILARY
MYRNA 1 & 2
JONATHAN
NATHALIE
NORA
KAREMA

SCENE LIST

INTRODUCTION
MICHELLE OBAMA ALWAYS SAYS IT BEST
THIS IS WHAT RESILIENCE SOUNDS LIKE
TONE DEAF AMERICA
WHAT I SEE HAPPENING AROUND ME (PART 1)
JUST…STOP. PLEASE
I AM ANGRY ALL OF THE DAMN TIME
WILL IT EVER END
THE SYSTEM
A PIECE OF MY WOMB
I HEAR YOU
STOP KILLING US
THE RIGHT THING TO DO
ARE MY PEOPLE OKAY?
SIMPLY TIRED
AFRICAN AMERICAN HUMANS
NOW?
TOP 10 REASONS WHY I AM SO TIRED OF BEING TIRED
STORIES THAT LEAVE SCARS
DESPITE BEING TIRED AND SCARRED, I AM HOPEFUL
WHAT I SEE HAPPENING ALL AROUND ME (PART 2)
WHAT THE PEOPLE HAVE TO SAY
MY EGO
WHAT I SEE HAPPENING ALL AROUND ME (PART 3)
CHANGE BEGINS WITH YOU
WHAT'S ON MY MIND
WHAT WILL MAKE THINGS BETTER
WE ARE STRONGER TOGETHER
LEARNING TO REST AND DISCONNECT IN MINNEAPOLIS
WHAT SIDE OF HISTORY WILL YOU BE ON?
CREATE CHANGE

BACKGROUND

June 2, 2020 - A friend of mine reached out to me in despair over her fear of being a person of color in today's social and political situation. Her message read, *Reaching out. I am crying between client calls. Please hold me in your thoughts. I have never been this scared, this vulnerable, as a person of color.*

A few days earlier, on May 25, 2020, George Floyd, a Black man in Minneapolis, Minnesota was murdered while being arrested. The arresting officer kneeled on his neck for almost nine minutes straight. Three other officers on the scene also kneeled on Mr. Floyd's body during the arrest. Protests began nationwide. White supremacist groups took advantage of the situation, inciting more chaos and destruction, posing as "Antifa." Local businesses were burned and looted. President Trump called in the National Guard and the Army to "dominate" the unrest. Social media lit up like a Christmas tree with posts from people telling their stories of fear, distrust, pain, sadness, and, most often, exhaustion. The calls for white people to assist and support started pouring in. It was time for real allyship to emerge.

Scrolling through Facebook, I started closely reading their often-traumatic stories. Wanting to do something effective, I started re-posting their stories on my own page so more people would read them. Over and over again, I'd read accounts and perspectives that were not my own but with whom I empathized, and found solidarity. I wanted to do something more. I wanted to use social media for good.

In our messaging, my friend asked, *Have you ever written your own play?* My first thought was, *uh...no. I direct plays - I don't WRITE them.* My second thought, *if I can do anything, maybe I can do THIS.*

I started to collect these stories from a wide variety of people whose lives had crossed paths with mine at some point, and they are all dear to me. Most are former students of mine from Spring Valley High School, part of the East Ramapo Central School District. About 97% of the public-school students there are people of color, many of whom experience poverty, are immigrants, and are desperate to find a better way to live. It is a community that is not unfamiliar with the inequities of racism and intolerance.

This piece exposes the feelings and responses in the aftermath of this pivotal point in American history of people who are of color and not of color, but who share the common belief that racism must be rooted out immediately and with impunity.

I would like to thank my brave friends who shared their bold narratives. Without them offering their deepest and most difficult thoughts, during a period of such uncertainty and unrest, this play would not exist. I am eternally grateful for their generosity of spirit and clarity of thought.

AUTHOR'S NOTES

Casting: The play is intended to have actors double-up on roles. Longer passages have been split up into smaller chunks so that no one actor has pages of dialogue to memorize. You can certainly choose to use one person for a longer passage - that is the director's choice. For the most part, the voices (unless specifically indicated) are voices of people of color. Obviously, different theatre groups have different casting pools. This shouldn't deter you from mounting the production, however it is extremely important that the narratives of people of color are presented from their perspective. Our first production had an all-female cast of 18.

While it goes without saying, I will say it anyway: NO BLACK FACE SHOULD EVER BE USED. Speaking as an ally, a kindred spirit, a supporter of those whose voices needs to be heard, I believe these roles can be done by a person who is not of color, as long as the performances are approached with respect for the experience of the characters. The roles of Hernz, Freddie, Andrew and Joe are the voices of Black males, but again the important takeaway is that you are telling their story, no matter who is playing the roles. You have some flexibility in casting the other roles, but the characters who are indicated as white should be approached from that perspective.

A note about the setting: this piece takes place during the COVID-19 pandemic that started in early 2020. We were in a global lockdown for an indeterminate amount of time, experienced social isolation, and never went anywhere without a protective mask. As we move further away from this time and find our way back to "normal," these concepts should be considered as you approach the direction of your production.

While you may not change the wording of the dialogue, you may decide to change the order of the passages. I think it works best as scripted, but a director might want to change the order for dramatic effect. Each passage represents an important facet in the expression of the complexities of racial injustice and must be performed as is.

The show can be performed with or without an intermission. The audience might need a break, especially within a school community, given the difficult nature of the material.

While the production is designed as a stage play, our first production was mounted during the 2020 pandemic, when much of our school year was done remotely. We created a virtual presentation for a limited release. Please obtain the correct licensing to do so if that is your desire for performance.

The song, "Now?" © 2020 by Stacey Tirro and Hernz Laguerre, Jr., should be licensed separately. Please contact Stacey Tirro for more information at stacey.tirro@gmail.com.

ACKNOWLEDGEMENTS

How Do We Feel Right Now? was first performed by Spring Valley High School's Thespian Troupe 721 on December 3, 2020 under the direction of Stacey Tirro with the following cast:

NARRATORS	Charlene Aurelus, Dinajah Green, Chelsy Louisthelmy
OBAMA NARRATOR	Jimna Aurelus
JULIE	Genesis Palma
JAEL	Jimna Aurelus
TATI 1 - 4	Ebony Nixon, Tatiana Gabriel, Jimna Aurelus, Chelsy Louisthelmy, Rivka Coffy
CHRIS	Jennifer Ojeda
DANA 1 & 2	Alison Porras, Anijah Smith
DARIAN	Anastasia Calixte
MAY	Genesis Palma
R.P.	Ani Jah Smith
KAYLA	Dinajah Green
JULIANNA	Jennifer Ojeda
STEPHANIE	Tatiana Gabriel
NADEGE	Jimna Aurelus
HERNZ	Kiara Pierristil, Anastasia Calixte, Ebony Nixon
FREDDIE 1 - 10	Ashley Amaning, Dinajah Green, Tatiana Gabriel, Khiara Worrell
ANDREW 1 - 4	Rivka Coffy, Charlene Aurelus, Briannah Marseille
JAIME	Ashley Amaning
JOE 1 - 3	Anijah Smith, Jimna Aurelus, Ebony Nixon
PAM	Tea Hubert, Alison Porras, Jennifer Ojeda
KIARA 1 - 7	Kiara Pierristil, Ashley Amaning
WHITE MALE FRIEND	Jennifer Ojeda
THE GIRLFRIEND	Briannah Marseille
ANOTHER VOICE	Dinajah Green
STEVEN	Alison Porras
LAURA	Tea Hubert
HILARY	Genesis Palma
MYRNA 1 & 2	Rivka Coffy, Briannah Marseille
JONATHAN	Alison Porras
NORA	Tea Hubert
KAREMA	Anastasia Calixte

10

"Now?" (song) was recorded and performed by special arrangement with Stacey Tirro and Hernz Laguerre, Jr.

Lead Vocal   Jimna Aurelus
Ensemble   Ashley Amaning, Charlene Aurelus, Rivka Coffy,
       Kiara Pierristil, Jennifer Ojeda, Alison Porras, Khiara Worrell

HOW DO WE FEEL RIGHT NOW?

by Stacey Tirro

ACT I

INTRODUCTION

NARRATOR #1: On May 25, 2020, George Floyd, a Black man in Minneapolis, Minnesota was murdered while being arrested. The arresting officer kneeled on his neck for almost nine minutes straight. Three other officers on the scene also kneeled on Mr. Floyd's body during the arrest. Protests began nationwide. White supremacist groups took advantage of the situation, inciting more chaos, confusion, and destruction, some posing as "Antifa." Riots broke out and local businesses and a police precinct were burned and looted. President Trump called in the National Guard and the Army to "dominate" the unrest. Social media lit up like a Christmas tree with posts by people telling their stories of fear, sadness, distrust, pain, and, most often, exhaustion. The calls for white people to assist and support by spreading the message about racial injustice started pouring in. It was time for real allyship to emerge.

NARRATOR #2: What you are about to see are first-hand responses - many expressed through social media pages, to the ongoing travesties that people of color live with every day. Some of the perspectives reflect difficult and intense feelings. You may agree or disagree with some of the statements, but they are actual, honest expressions from real people in the initial weeks following the death of Mr. Floyd. The most important takeaway from this piece is that for people who live in skin that is some shade of brown, the feelings expressed here *never go away*. The expressions may get quieter, but they are never gone. If you feel like they *have* gone away, or that you just don't see it, that might just be your privilege talking.

NARRATOR #3: We invite you to open your heart, open your mind, and hear what people are feeling. Then, consider how you can choose to help.

MICHELLE OBAMA ALWAYS SAYS IT BEST

NARRATOR: On Tuesday, October 29 2019, former First Lady Michelle Obama spoke at the Obama Foundation Summit in her hometown of Chicago. One particular quote speaks volumes:

> *I can't make people not afraid of Black people. I don't know what's going on. I can't explain what's happening in your head. But maybe if I show up every day as a human, a good human, doing wonderful things, loving my family, loving your kids, taking care of things that I care about—maybe, just maybe that work will pick away at the scabs of your discrimination. Maybe that slowly will unravel it. That's all we have, because we can't do it for them, because they're broken. Their brokenness in how they see us is a reflection of this brokenness. And you can't fix that. All you can do is the work.*

The work that we believe Mrs. Obama is referring to, is about taking an honest, deep look into what people are feeling, and how they are responding. This piece is our interpretation of that work.

THIS IS WHAT RESILIENCE SOUNDS LIKE

JULIE: May 28, 2020 - Checking in on those whose hearts and minds are heavy this morning.

You are so not alone. When you feel helpless about George Floyd's murder in Minneapolis, exhale. Remember that you are still alive and can do something. You must find a way to keep moving forward.

Yes, we can.

To my white friends, don't keep your understanding of injustice to yourself. You must do something with it. Those of you who have been doing this for your entire lives, yes, I know you are tired. I am, too. Do take care of yourself. We need you. I need you.

To my Black friends, I wasn't color blind. I saw your skin and I saw you. Most of the Black friends I grew up with in Spring Valley, New York were first generation Haitian or Jamaican. Your parents immigrated to the States around the same time as mine. I practiced with you on the ballfields, pushed you on the swings and ran with you on the playground. I sang with you in chorus, played with you in orchestra, and ate with you in the lunchroom. I passed notes to you in class, talked on the phone with you after school and had sleepovers. Your parents drove us to the movies, helped us with our science project, and gave us snacks. I met you at your lockers, rehearsed with you for the spring musical, and danced with you at prom.

I see you still, my friends. And I love you.

June 1, 2020: What does "I am not okay" mean? For me, it means that my world is exploding. It's as if every pain I have ever felt is coming back to haunt me. I am scared and I am sad. I am grieving that we still don't get it, after decades and decades and decades of supposed lessons learned. My heart aches and I am struggling to breathe.

But I refuse to give up, Mr. DuBois, Mr. Douglass, Ms. Wells, Dr. King, Ms. Lorde, Malcolm, Ms. Morrison, Ms. Hurston, and Mr. Hughes. I learned too much from you to not to try to help communities heal. I refuse to give up, friends, I refuse to give up, Mom. I refuse to give up, Dad.

I refuse to give up.

TONE-DEAF AMERICA

JAEL: How do I feel right now? I haven't had a decent night of sleep for about a week now. I am saddened, frustrated, confused, at a loss for words but yet have so much to say. I am frustrated with the people that think anti-police brutality is "anti-cops." I am annoyed with people that keep saying "all lives matter." Because if all lives matter then why don't Black lives matter?

I am tired of explaining to tone-deaf America why I'm afraid for my brother, dad, and cousins every day when they leave their homes. I'm baffled to see how much hate that we have to deal with *still to this day*.

Above all, I'm thankful for my non-Black friends and acquaintances that are speaking out against such treatments. Thank you for using your voice and platforms to drive out hate, racial profiling and police brutality. I love you all from the bottom of my heart. I feel your love and support. I'm in tears as I'm typing this. Love conquers hate - always.

WHAT I SEE HAPPENING AROUND ME (PART 1)

TATI 1: Growing up, I experienced racism, colorism, and sexism. I always thought that if a boy could lift three chairs, then I could lift four. If my light-skinned friend can play with a group of other light-skinned kids then I can too. If a Caucasian man can get pulled over by the police, show his license and registration and go home with just a warning, then I can too. I wish I still had this mentality. Knowing that Black men, women and children are being treated unfairly around America makes me feel powerless. I don't understand why people are being biased towards skin color. I shouldn't have to wonder about whether I'll make it back home alive after going to get a bag of chips from the store.

TATI 2: Growing up I hated my skin color because at school I would hear people call my other classmates with darker skin complexion "burnt," and other hurtful names. I felt lesser than the lighter-skinned kids. I would chemically burn my hair straight because I hated having coily 4C hair. I rarely ever saw famous people that looked like me back then so I felt ugly. However, I have grown to realize that Black is beautiful.

TATI 3: There are protests going on about being equal to each other because of how police officers are treating people of color all around the world. All states in America are having protests. A specific protest that sticks out to me is the one in D.C. President Donald Trump hid in a bunker and decided to turn a peaceful protest violent because he wanted to take a picture in front of a church with a bible. He made the officers shoot rubber bullets, tear gas and arrest protesters. These people were unarmed and being peaceful, so why did they attack them? I think the government is abusing their power. Their right to protest and speak freely is protected under the First Amendment. So why are they [the government] going against people's constitutional right? This quote from Cornell Law School's Legal Information Institute explains this right: (*shown on-screen*)

> *The most basic component of freedom of expression is the right to freedom of speech. Freedom of speech may be exercised in a direct (words) or a symbolic (actions) way. Freedom of speech is recognized as a human right under article 19 of the Universal Declaration of Human Rights. The right to freedom*

of speech allows individuals to express themselves without government interference or regulation.

TATI 4: The coronavirus seems to have gone away from the media because of the protests. The most recent news that I've heard was that camps might be able to open in the summer. I miss my friends and I'm tired of being home. Quarantine really has negative effects on people's minds. I've been getting sick because of lack of sunlight and movement, but my whole body hurts like I ran a marathon. I can't wait 'til this quarantine is lifted.

The year 2020 will definitely be in history books because of the events that have occurred. I hope this madness ends by September because I don't want my senior year to get messed up. All we can do is sit and wait for what will happen next.

JUST...STOP. PLEASE

CHRIS *(who is white)*: If I see one more white person post some meme about Martin Luther King, Jr. never rioting, my head may explode. All that peaceful protesting *got him assassinated by a white man*!! The irony and ignorance is astonishing.

Also, I'm tired of being shown pictures of white cops being nice to Black children, as if that balances things out. We all know that happens. We all already cling to the hope that there is more good than bad out there. What we need to see is white cops standing up to other white cops and calling them out for their racism. Show us pictures and videos of that. The good cops need to take a stand against some of their own. Now. Or else all that effort they put into making their communities better places will have been wasted.

Stop shaming people. Stop looking for ways to keep doing things the way they've always been done. Just...stop. Please.

I AM ANGRY ALL OF THE DAMN TIME

DANA 1: I wish white and non-Black evangelical Trump supporters and sympathizers could feel for ten measly seconds the kind of complete, destructive brokenness I felt after he was elected. The instant rage I feel whenever I hear his voice, see his face, read his words. The complete terror and fear I feel when I read how the folks in and out of my life support him or look on the "bright side" or are slow to condemn him.

To me, he is a racist and he is incompetent, and it is so upsetting that people choose not to understand, not to believe why I am so angry, and that they actively work to invalidate my feelings and experiences. Instead of listening to the reality of Black Americans' distress, I see people creating their own narrative to rationalize and dismiss that pain, and really, it is so UN-Jesus-like that it breaks my spirit. I have felt so incomplete since those election results, like a ghost of myself. I am angry all of the damn time. It is my constant condition. And I cannot let it go. I will not let it go until this man starts getting held accountable - and I mean *really* held accountable - for his actions and words.

DANA 2: Some of y'all really cling so hard to controlling so many aspects of other people's lives - things YOU deem as "sinful" - that you will excuse the continuous sins of the President of the United States. Are leaders not called to a higher standard? Would you make the same excuses for your pastor? Your elders? Whatever happened to leaders being held accountable for their actions?

It is all such a shame. I am beyond disappointed. Was then. Still am now. And sadly, will likely continue to be.

Oh, and while we are here, please do understand that the body should be held accountable too. I have had racist things said and done to me within the church. Things that made me feel so isolated and are part of the reason why I keep to myself in most cases today. And while there are folks who I care about and who I know care about me within the body - it shouldn't take my constant cries for folks to understand that *I am hurting*. My family *is hurting*. I may smile for you, talk about other subjects, but make no mistake we are in pain. And for me, the silence I felt over the years, from Trayvon Martin, to Sandra Bland, Michael Brown, Ferguson, Charlottesville, Ahmaud Arbery, Breonna Taylor, George Floyd etc. etc., that silence - not from all but from so many - feels like a slap in the face. And boy does it sting.

WILL IT EVER END

DARIAN: I am tired.

(She is reading the paper. The headlines show on a screen, or are heard in a voiceover. She reacts to each headline with more frustration.)

"Florida police officer put on leave after pinning Black man to the ground with knee"

"Alabama police officer cleared in shooting of Black man at mall"

"Police fatally shoot a Brooklyn man, saying they thought he had a gun"

"Arizona man claims he killed teen because victim's rap music made him feel 'unsafe'"

ALTERNATING ACTORS *(Voice overs)*: Trayvon Martin. Eric Garner. Michael Brown. Tamir Rice. Sandra Bland. Philando Castile. Ahmaud Arbery. Breonna Taylor. George Floyd.

DARIAN: My heart hurts. I am afraid. I am scared to run in my neighborhood. I fear crossing paths with the police.

But most of all, I am terrified of having children - not because of the pains of labor but because I would have to protect them from a world that sees them as a threat and treats their lives as expendable.

Because I would have to give them "The Talk" - not about the birds and the bees, but about the harsh reality that in a country that promises liberty and justice for all, there is no liberty and justice for us. Because I would hold my breath every time they left the safety of our home. Because just being Black puts them at risk.

My mind is troubled. I am angry. "All Lives Matter," they say. Not when Black people are exterminated by the people that swore to protect and serve. "Violence doesn't solve anything," they say. Yeah, tell that to your ancestors. "Not all cops are bad cops," they say. Well, in the words of Ginetta Sagan, "silence in the face of injustice is complicity with the oppressor."

So miss me with that crap! My blood boils. When will it end? Will it ever end?

THE SYSTEM

JAIME: I think it's also worth looking at being anti-system versus anti-person. It doesn't matter if there are good cops, it doesn't matter what truth is in anyone's heart. What matters is that the entire system is leading to racist outcomes. *The system enables the murder of Black people and protects the perpetrators, and that's what needs to change.*

A PIECE OF MY WOMB

R.P..: During this time, it has only further proven, solidified, and supported my husband's and my decisions to not bring Black children into this world. This world doesn't deserve a piece of my womb, and it wouldn't be fair to bring a beautiful Black child somewhere that I know is evil. I cannot protect them.

I fear becoming a widow at any moment, at the hands of police brutality, especially living in a "white area," and I prepare for that fatal call. But being a single mother or a mother who has to bury her child - I don't have the strength for that.

I HEAR YOU

MAY: As I try to find words to express my thoughts and feelings at this difficult time, I am at a loss to find those words that would do justice to convey the ideal message. Mostly, I wish I could hug my dear students, friends, members of the community, and let them know I see you, I hear you, I support you, I am here for you, I love you. My hope is that together we can make the world a better place.

STOP KILLING US

KAYLA: I've dealt with racism all of my life - racist jokes from someone at my school, someone calling me a "f-ing nigger" *(bleep if necessary)* in a store, and I'm sure it will never stop. There's not much more that I can say other than *stop killing us*. Support your Black friends and family today and every day. Donate to Black-owned businesses, protest peacefully, cry, and scream. I'm here with you, and for you.

THE RIGHT THING TO DO

JULIANNA *(who is white)*: What if I told you "all lives don't matter" until Black ones do.... Simply put, they are part of the "all." Think of it this way. Three children are swimming. One starts to drown. Everyone is gonna help that child, yes? Does that mean that the other two beautiful children don't matter? Nope. It's just who needs our help, compassion, love and support at that time. The right thing to do, whether it's your child or not, is to help... yes? That's why white people are saying 'Black Lives Matter.' Do we have the "right color" to be in this game? No. But we can speak out, stand in solidarity with them, never settle for less - not for us, for them. It's the best way I've thought of to explain. Think about it that way. The words can sound one-sided, but in reality, that's not what it means. Love everyone. Take your love, smile, kindness, sprinkle it around like confetti.

ARE MY PEOPLE OKAY?

STEPHANIE: Are my brothers okay? Are my parents okay? Are my cousins okay? Are my friends okay? I run through a roll call, a list in my head of my loved ones, and check in. It's something I usually do, but even more so now.

I knew that I was different growing up, different than a lot of kids in a lot of ways. Being a first generation Haitian American, I grew up knowing that I needed to work twice as hard to be successful and was taught that it was the only way to success. I was also taught the importance of treating everyone with respect, being friendly, and doing your best.

When I personally experienced racism for the first time, I was incredibly shaken up. I couldn't identify that what was taking place was racism at first.

The older I get, the more and more I understand why my parents didn't allow my brothers and me to go outside. Growing up, we were inside playing video games, reading, watching TV and rarely going outside to "hang out with friends." My parents were always concerned about our safety and felt safest and most secure when we were all under the same roof. I see the same look of relief and smiles that overcome their faces when my adult brothers and I are all at home to visit. I see my brothers as loving, gentle, nerdy musical geniuses. To the world, they're just Black men, a potential threat. Our skin is seen as a threat. And yet we operate in the world with a welcoming smile.

We enter spaces where we're more than likely to be the only Black person or one of a few and have to take on the weight of feeling as though we speak for all of them. We also have to walk the line of fitting in so we don't stand out too much.

I understand why my mom can't sleep. I understand why my dad, the gentle giant he is, tells us that we need to be cool, breathe and be nice. The older I get, the more enraged and tired I get.

SIMPLY TIRED

NADEGE: I'm angry that this is all even happening. Frustrated that we even have to fight for our right to live. Scared because the pessimistic side of me only sees this getting worse. Sad because I know people are dying. But above all, I'm simply tired of having to use analogies and metaphors to explain why Black Lives Matter, as if the concept of a Black life mattering is some sort of complex theory or formula.

I'm tired of watching videos of Black men, Black women and Black children being killed by police and white supremacists. I'm tired of people trying to justify the killings and minimizing the importance of human lives. I'm tired of the blatant and deeply rooted racism this society has made exceptions and excuses for time and time again. I'm tired of crying over another hashtag. I'm tired of being told to go back to Africa if we don't like it here. I'm tired of being silenced. And I refuse to be silent anymore.

I'm ready for things to change. I'm ready for Black lives to be *valued*. I'm ready for people to stop dehumanizing us. I'm ready to be loud and obnoxious if that's what it takes to be heard. I'm ready to destroy the roots of racism and hatred in this country so that when I finally have children, I can be positive that the whole world knows that their lives matter.

AFRICAN AMERICAN HUMANS

PAM *(who is white)*

PAM 1: This madness needs to stop. I was brought up at a time that most of my friends were African American humans. My best friend was a beautiful smart African American human. My high school was mostly African American humans. We respected each other, we sang in choir together, we played on the field together, we marched in band together, we studied in class together, we went on field trips together, we graduated together. My dad's best buddy was a kind African American human, who came over for BBQ, with his whole family.

PAM 2: In Roselle, where I grew up, was a town of diversity. Our police officers were mostly white. Everyone got along and helped each other - without violence, without tear gas, without guns, without protests. Black lives mattered, but not without our help and respect and compassion. We don't need guns to protect us, or protests that turn violent. We need action and conversation - peaceful conversation. The rhetoric is too much and dangerous. Protecting our children, all American humans, is by education; having those tough conversations with them.

PAM 3: We are Americans, plain and simple, no matter what race, ethnicity, faith, or by the choices that we make in how we live our lives. Justice will be done to those who have killed these American humans. So inhuman. This police brutality needs to be dealt with. I have known so many good and respectful police officers throughout my life. My friend is the best one I know. This racism has been an ongoing pandemic. Have the conversations *now*. We are all American humans.

NOW?

HERNZ 1:
Did you see...
Did you hear...
Did you listen...
Why did you sleep so long?
Days and decades passed since you first hit that snooze button.
Centuries filled with generations that were affected as you dreamt
Sound asleep...as we screamed

Drooling on pillows...as blood was spilt

HERNZ 2:
Did you see me...
Did you hear me...
Did you listen to me...
When the chaos got loud you drowned out the noise with your pillow
When the flames got bright outside you pulled your blinds
From the old slaves jumping ship drowning in their sorrow and anguish
To the new slaves being robbed blind of an opportunity of a fair life....
You were asleep

HERNZ 3:
Did you see me hurting?
Did you hear me calling out to you?
Did you listen to me crying out?
Distractions
A lot of distractions
You're in a room full of distractions
but at a drop of a dime, you can drop all of your distractions
You choose to keep them...and proceed on being distracted
Mumbled noise from the outside but you focused on them distractions
You chose to ignore
You did see me, but you couldn't be bothered.
You heard me call your name, but you were preoccupied.
You were listening but tuned me out when I tried to explain what's going on.

(Actors alternate the following lines)
Things have changed in light of recent events and
I appreciate everyone who is finally
Standing up,
Showing up,
Speaking up,
Reading up,
But Listen up,
I find it messed up
(ALL) that you are finally awake...now.

End of Act One

ACT II

TOP 10 REASONS WHY I AM SO TIRED OF BEING TIRED

FREDDIE 10: Having to define privilege, and explain the difference between racism and prejudice.

FREDDIE 9: Being told I'm over-thinking racist incidents, or having my pain misinterpreted, because most folks chose to focus on their discomfort by not discussing or acknowledging racism, fear and prejudice. These conversations are usually followed by silence and labeling.

FREDDIE 8: Telling people not to insult people of color by calling them *minorities*, a term that is defined in the dictionary as "less than equal," introduced to the American vernacular by politicians, to lump those they consider less important, together under one heading, and subconsciously teaching folks of color to dismiss themselves.

FREDDIE 7: Racist parents teaching their children to fear my brown skin. Women clutching their purses and pocketbooks as Black men pass by their shopping carts or enter the elevators they occupy. White people meeting you for the first time and telling you that from your prior phone conversations that you didn't "sound Black."

FREDDIE 6: Seeing car windows being closed and doors locked as Black men walk through parking lots to their car, even when holding the hand of their small child. Or, noticing white folks crossing the street to avoid them out of fear, and then crossing back after they pass.

FREDDIE 5: Black men learning early in life that Black men are perceived as intimidating and overcompensating and going out of their way to be nice because they feel they have to comfort white people.

FREDDIE 4: When it has to be explained to white men that even though you look athletic, your lifelong dream is not to fulfill some white coach's fantasy by playing football and basketball in college, but instead enjoying non-stereotypical sports.

FREDDIE 3: When people question Black men's support of the police, even when many grew up with police officers in their family. And even when that is the case, they are taught by their parents to fear the police due to the unjust murders by bad cops.

FREDDIE 2: Being pulled over for driving a new car while Black and panicking that as a Black man, you may not survive the encounter. Or looking over your shoulder when you go out for a run. Or that wearing a hoodie while running might, in fact, be a death sentence.

FREDDIE 1: Always being hopeful while praying for a better world for you and your children.

(ALL) And this just scratches the surface.

STORIES THAT LEAVE SCARS

ANDREW 1: I have a high school memory of walking from my school to the train station only to be greeted by a very tall white police officer, who would psychologically intimidate my friends of color and me about using our train passes. He would then tell us on a regular basis, that he didn't know "why they let us "[insert racial slurs here] go to school out here in this white neighborhood. We don't want you here, and one day I just may throw one of you little [racial slurs] on the third rail to watch you fry." I was fourteen.

ANDREW 2: My high school guidance counselor tried to convince me not to take Honors chemistry and my true love, AP studio art, because she felt I should take a class to teach me how to use a cash register and develop basic business skills instead: "great jobs for minorities." She told me I should consider careers like those in the Sanitation Department because at the time she said it was paying $22K, and I was a big, strong, young Black man. Of course, my mother was really upset but as a single parent could not take off from work to go fight the fight. Thank God I defied her and was accepted to a competitive university at sixteen.

ANDREW 3: I took a coaching certification class in the evening at a local high school. On a break I went to use the bathroom. A white mother with her daughter approached me in the hallway to tell me that they had spilled something by the door upon entering the building and it needed to be cleaned up before someone slipped. For that moment, I was the speechless Black custodian. I chose to hold in my disgust and anger because she was with her young child and did not understand her racist ignorance, assuming that I, the Black man, was the custodian.

Had I opened my mouth to express my feelings, I may have been labeled as the angry and aggressive big Black man.

ANDREW 4: I had to convince my child that she earned the right to be in her AP European history class. She had been told by her white classmates that being Black, they questioned her placement in the class as a Black girl (she was the only person of color). Adding insult to injury, whenever a question about race or people of color arose, both the teacher and her classmates looked for her input as the "authority on Black people" in the discussions.

DESPITE BEING TIRED AND SCARRED, I AM HOPEFUL

JOE 1: I see people of all races marching to support justice for these senseless murders and to call out racism. I wonder - will the system hold the murderers and bad cops accountable, or will they continue to cloud the press with empty promises and distractions until cases run cold? Because of the recent horrific murders of Black men and women, more of my friends and colleagues are now demonstrating a willingness to understand the pain of racism, white privilege, and why Black lives *have* to matter.

JOE 2: Historically, I have noticed that not all Asian, Latin, or Black folks want to align themselves with their history and the existence of racism. Unfortunately, too many of my friends from all races still remain silent and therefore, complicit. I celebrate the vocal ones because in their hearts they are choosing to try to understand the pain. We already see the news cycle changing, and people on social media are hoping they no longer have to see Black Lives Matter posts about injustice. The TV news stations have started to reduce reporting on the protests that continue nationally, while the police are still arresting and violating individuals' civil rights.

JOE 3: Do not be confused by my fatigue. My ancestors that were murdered and enslaved, and experienced a holocaust of over 20 million in the middle passage did so, so I would have the right to be tired and educated. They have inspired in me the determination to fight, to march, to teach, to challenge, to question, and to continue the quest of "Justice for All" in this stolen land.

WHAT I SEE HAPPENING ALL AROUND ME (PART 2)

(In the background, an actress representing Kiara will animate the speech and interact with the WHITE MALE FRIEND)

KIARA 1: I was on the phone with a friend yesterday when a notification popped on my screen. It said: *(shows on screen)* "Curfew in New York from 7 p.m. until 6 a.m." I immediately told my friend that he should probably get back home because I just found out that the president had instituted a curfew. He said to me:

WHITE MALE FRIEND: "It's whatever. If there is really a curfew, the worst that could happen is that a cop will drive me back home."

KIARA 1: I was about to protest in an attempt to convince him to get back home, but it hit me. I realized that he was right and that a cop driving him back home was the worst that could happen because he is a 14-year-old white male.

I laughed so hard and started pacing hysterically because I realized that my older cousin, who was supposed to be home hours ago wasn't, and that he hadn't and no one in the house had heard from him. My father called home and asked if the curfew was real. He wanted to know so he could figure out a way to get back home unharmed after his shift at the bakery. Later on, around one o'clock, my cousin was dropped off in front of the house. He told us that he had to wait at the hospital for his girlfriend to pick him up because she didn't want him taking the risk of getting back home alone.

THE GIRLFRIEND: "A young Black man in the streets after curfew did not paint the right picture."

KIARA 1: My father also made it home safely. I was never as relieved to see both of them as I was that day.

KIARA 2: The past few weeks have been the hardest of my life so far. There has never been a more dangerous time to be a Black person in America. I look around and I see riots, protests and pain everywhere. The irony and the injustice of the situation has me going around in circles asking myself, "Is that the world that I am fighting so hard to live in?" The people who are supposed to protect us have turned on us. We, the Black people of America, have to now watch out for cops, racist groups and gang members alike.

I am disgusted by everything that is going on. The fact that Black people have to protest and break things to be heard in this country is outrageous. I always believed that violence is never the way to get what you want, and I still do, but the fact that the government only started to pay attention to the protests when they turned into riots is mind-blowing. I saw a post that said:

ANOTHER ACTOR: "They would rather arrest a hundred Black men for demanding justice instead of arresting four of their own."

KIARA 2: And that hit hard. It pains me that we live in a world where Black people are still treated as less than human and that white privilege is still a thing.

KIARA 3: The news of George Floyd's death and all of these other Black people, may they rest in peace, reminded me of the movie "The Hate U Give." In that movie, a Black kid was pulled over and killed by a white cop because he thought that the kid was holding a weapon. Later in the movie, his friend asked her uncle, who is a cop, if he were in the same circumstances as the cop that had killed her friend - but instead of a Black man, the kid was white - what would he have done? The uncle answered, "I would've said, 'put your hands up.'"

Like the kid in the movie, many other young Black men have been killed by white cops, because they thought that they had weapons. Unlike those people, George Floyd was unarmed and pinned to the ground. He died under the knee of a white cop pressed to his throat while saying, "I can't breathe."

KIARA 4: Despite everything that is happening, I remain proud to be Black. I am also proud to see all the solidarity and the support we get from other people in our fight for justice. The Black Lives Matter movement has never been as popular as it is right now. I just wish that people would remember that yes, Black lives do matter - all the time, not only when one of us is killed.

I pray that one day these unjust acts cease and that I will be able to stop pacing every time one of my relatives is an hour late. I pray that one day I will be able to tell my friends "see you tomorrow" instead of "be careful" every time I leave their sides. I pray that one day Black people won't have to resort to violence to be heard, and that a Black man won't need a white person to step in front of him and shield him from potential harm.

WHAT THE PEOPLE HAVE TO SAY

STEVEN *(who is white)*: Tens of thousands of protesters trying to get across their message and there are those who continue to focus solely on the rioters and looters; man, it's almost as if they have absolutely no interest in hearing what the people have to say.

Should a white person have to answer for the actions of all white people? If your answer is no, why in the hell should a Black person have to answer for the actions of all Black people?

Everyone just wants to go about their lives in peace and to be treated fairly. Jerks come in every color. Let's start focusing on recognizing everyone's humanity and we can then move forward from there.

MY EGO

LAURA *(who is white)*: I am trying very hard not to "white" over Black voices. I am trying very hard to use my profile as a megaphone to amplify Black voices. If I fail in this or if I minimize Black voices and experiences, let me know. My ego should not ever get in the way of your voice.

WHAT I SEE HAPPENING ALL AROUND ME (PART 3)

KIARA 5: I was only a kid when my mother taught me about the civil rights movement. She told me about Martin Luther King and Rosa Parks. I did not fully understand then but I could tell that she was passionate and so proud. Later, I studied Dr. King in history books. I was amazed and proud to be part of such a great culture. I was proud of my brothers and sisters in America for fighting for their rights and justice. Now, 64 years later, we still fight for those rights. I wonder, what would those people think, if they were here now.

There is a famous line from the movie "The Hate U Give" which states: "It is impossible to be unarmed when our Blackness is the weapon they fear."

These lines have never rung more true in my mind than in the last two weeks. In the past couple of days, I have seen Black men get frisked by white cops for walking in a parking lot. I have heard of a Black man getting shot for standing in the corner of a street. I have seen and heard my brother die under the knee of a white cop while saying: "I can't breathe!"

KIARA 6:   In what world does using a fake twenty-dollar bill deserve murder as punishment? In what world does one need three other people kneeling on a man's body to restrain him? Since when did the ones who have pledged to protect and serve us, have turned on us?

I never thought that I would see the day when my Blackness would be the reason why I end up dead. I never thought that I would fear for my family's life like I do now every time they walk out the door. I never thought that I would doubt whether or not calling the cops was the best thing to do if I was ever in danger.

I watched a video of a woman, on TikTok, telling her elderly grandfather that African Americans were still fighting for justice in America. The man cried and responded: "I thought we had the time to fix that."

KIARA 7: I saw a cop push an elderly white man to the ground while he was in a protest. His skull cracked open and his blood spilled on the ground, yet the cops walked past. It was as if none of them saw the poor man bleeding out of his head! I have seen the worst and the best of humanity in the past few days, and I have never shed more tears.

I have seen white people fight and stand with us for justice. I have seen a nation march united, asking for justice and fight against the oppressor, and I am proud. I am proud of the people for standing and fighting the good fight. I am relieved for their support. I pray that this time there will be a lasting change, and that 64 years from now, my descendants will not be shedding the same tears as I am; that they will not be fighting the same fight that we have been fighting for decades.

CHANGE BEGINS WITH YOU

HILARY *(who is white)*: I've been trying to find the right words for what is going on in our country. I'm horrified, sad, discouraged, frustrated, enraged, disappointed, and flummoxed. My heart hurts. Judging someone by the color of their skin is *wrong*. There isn't *any* situation where it is appropriate.

We as a country, need to find a way to eradicate racism and that starts with each of us. I will combat those that disagree with this. I will teach my future children how to accept everyone. Change begins with you.

WHAT'S ON MY MIND

MYRNA 1: Facebook asks "what's on my mind?" Today, here's what's on my mind. I woke up Thursday morning knowing I wasn't okay. This is what I felt:

- It's okay to not be okay.
- It's okay to need people and share my heart with them.
- There's a lot going on in the world, and in *my* world.
- I've met all that with more anxiety than I know how to deal with, so it's wreaking havoc on my mind.
- My silence is simply me trying to process what is happening. Or, it's just me being tired.
- It's okay to lean on God fully through this.
- It doesn't make a bit of sense to me, but this is bigger than me.

I couldn't sleep last night.

Saying the wrong thing is a core fear. And not all people are kind. The way *some* folks react and attack others for saying the "wrong" thing or the right thing the "wrong" way *scares* me. So, I listened, I watched, and honestly was filled with encouragement at how many people have shown up and *how* they've shown up. I've appreciated the vulnerability and honesty shared by so many.

Also, I have just been confused. Y'all, nothing has changed. We have been living with systemic oppression since before I was born. I've been trying to figure out what in the world was different now. Why are so many now finally "showing up?" I think part of it is social media. Maybe the other part is we're tired. I know I'm tired. But clearly something is different. Pandemic?

MYRNA 2: When this whole quarantine started and schools closed, all I could think about is the education gap. The achievement gap. All I could think about were the kids. Do y'all realize how much wider the achievement gap has gotten? Do you recognize the disparity happening for our children of color across America in this very moment? Do you understand how many more of our students are now even *more* at risk of being a statistic in our school-to-prison pipeline? I'm sure you do. These are rhetorical questions that I literally just cannot fathom.

In my little corner of the world, I take a stand for our children to equip them to be successful in whatever path they choose, teaching them the realities of the world we live in and maintaining a high level of culturally relevant pedagogy so that just maybe they can have a chance.

Personally, I'm a Haitian American woman. In America, I'm perceived as a Black female. I'm blessed to have a diverse community with deep relationships across cultural lines.

But I'm a Black female. Point. Blank. Period.

That identity places me smack dab in the middle of so many systems of oppression. Being Black elicits one form of oppression; being female brings another. In that space of intersectionality, there are natural limitations, disadvantages, and/or disapprovals. And that junk is hard.

Then, there are my siblings. Specifically, I have two Black brothers. When some folks look at my older brother, they are automatically threatened by his stature. But, gosh, that dude is a teddy bear and his smile lights up your world for days. Legit the best smile ever. And my other brother has the most tender heart with his nerdy techie self. He's legit a life saver in so many ways. Neither are threats in the slightest - they love you in the purest way they know how.

(both) So, I'm tired.

1: Tired of watching so many Black Americans work twice as hard for half as much.

2: Tired of the conversations parents have to have with their Black children, especially their Black sons.

1: Tired that my fellow mommas who have Black sons choose to cut their sons' precious locks because they hit an age where it's no longer cute and is perceived as a threat.

2: Tired that we have to question our every move to ensure we're not putting ourselves in danger.

1: Tired of the pressure to act a certain way.

2: Tired that we have to fight this hard.

1: Tired that my babies have to fight even harder.

2: Tired that at the end of the day, all these systems of oppression are making it *even* harder for my babies to get a quality education and that the institutions and organizations that have set out to impact change for these communities are the very ones struggling during this pandemic.

MYRNA 1: So I pray hard for my family, my babies, the achievement gap, the systems of oppression. I pray and I focus my fight against injustice on influencing and impacting students because they are our future.

MYRNA 2: What's your part in the fight against injustice? You don't have to have the answers. You don't even have to fully understand the problem. You just need to be willing to show up, engage in conversation, be willing to grow, and impact others to do the same.

WHAT WILL MAKE THINGS BETTER

JONATHAN *(who is white)*: I've been so hesitant to post anything. I've wanted to but haven't. Here's what's gone through my mind - right, wrong or indifferent. What am I going to say that doesn't sound cliche?

That I went to a high school that was 50% people of color when I was there and all most of us cared about was what kind of teammate, classmate or coworker someone was regardless of what they looked like? It's true, but that isn't going to make things better.

That I have Black friends? I do, but that isn't going to make things better.

That I feel for the pain of people whom I know didn't grow up with the opportunities I had? I do, but that isn't going to make things better.

That I feel all cops aren't bad, but the ones who killed George Floyd deserve to rot in hell? I do, but that isn't going to make things better.

That while I don't agree with looting and violence, I know MLK, Tommie Smith, John Carlos, Colin Kaepernick and many others all tried different ways to get people's attention and still nothing has changed? I do, but that isn't going to make things better.

That I couldn't give two hoots if you are Black, brown, purple, gay, straight, trans or from Mars, as long as you are a good person (and teach my kids the same)? I do, but that isn't going to make things better.

The best thing I felt I could do was continue living the way I do, which means treating others with the dignity and respect they deserve. I didn't want to artificially call attention to it by being the white guy from the suburbs trying to seem woke to something I could never fully understand without experiencing it myself but know I never will. Maybe this is the wrong approach, but that's why I've chosen to be silent - well, with this reply perhaps I no longer am.

WE ARE STRONGER TOGETHER

NATHALIE: I want to give a shout out to two white firemen who stood up for me and this other Black young lady. In a nutshell, an older gentleman purposefully cut me in line, and even after both us women kindly told him there was a line, he looked at the both of us and rudely dismissed us! One of the firemen repeated it more firmly for the rude white man to get the point. He grudgingly moved. This is what happens when white privileged people hold other white privileged people, who are clearly racists, accountable. My white friends, do not be a bystander but stand up for the Black community.

The firemen even waited for the man to leave, grabbed my food for me, *and* waited for me to get in my car. It's getting messier in our world today. Yes, we need to pray, but actions speak louder than words. Let's continue to do what is right and be there for one another.

#callitlikeitis
#Blacklivesmatter
#wearestrongertogether
#totallycouldhavebeenworse

LEARNING TO REST AND DISCONNECT IN MINNEAPOLIS (6/4/2020)

NORA *(who is white)*: We've all heard the saying, "It takes a village to raise a child."

My dissertation affirmed that to have our social, emotional, spiritual, and physical needs met, we need to belong to a community that acts as a web of support. In my work at Inspire to Change, we say that there is no healthy collective transformative change without supporting individual and collective well-being.

And I learned through my work with The Wellbeing Project that well-being requires that people be able to rest and disconnect. Rest and disconnection are more likely to happen if people feel held by the community, and if they feel like the work will continue in their absence. It's a shift away from hero or savior models and the feeling that "I can't stop because this all rests on *my* shoulders," to "I can rest because I have people I trust who will keep fighting the good fight in my absence."

So, what is sufficient community? How big is a "web of support"? What do people actually do to "hold" each other? I'm going to make our web of support visible by listing things people have done to hold us.

In my community, people have:

(Actors alternate saying the following...)

1: Given us money so we could evacuate our home with the kids for the four most dangerous nights

2: Sent us grocery money and dropped off meals

3: Taken our son for socially distanced play dates

4: Watched our neighborhood throughout the night as protectors and peacekeepers

5: Checked in to ask, "How are you doing? What do you need?"

6: Checked in to say, "I'm reading what you are writing. I see you. I hear you. I appreciated you."

7: Created art in our community

8: Helped us get our story out beyond Minneapolis

9: Protested when we couldn't

10: Offered to run errands for us and our neighbors

11: Helped with neighborhood clean-up

12: Shared resources with me, and shared resources I've posted with others

13: Placed our son's social and emotional needs before academic performances

14: Filmed live footage, unfiltered by mainstream media so we could see what is happening while staying in and protecting our home

15: Helped synthesize the news while it was happening

16: Offered to keep watch with us at night

17: Offered us a place to stay

18: Kept work at Inspire to Change going when we couldn't concentrate

19: Sent random messages of love

20: Sent art

WHAT SIDE OF HISTORY WILL YOU BE ON?

KAREMA: I am Black. I am my ancestors' dreams. I am educated. I am an educator. I am an officer's daughter (worth mentioning for context). I am a proud product of the East Ramapo Central School District. I am fortunate to have grown up in a community with such diversity. It gave me depth. I am not afraid to challenge or lead. I am and will continue to be a trailblazer; a champion for children.

So, yesterday I protested for the first time with friends I've had since elementary school because it's bigger than all of us. The movement feels different this time around; similarly, to when Emmett Till's mom left his casket open for the world to see what racism did to her son. I am so proud to take part in a historic movement as such. We're at a turning point. I've always felt obligated to use my voice to empower our future, plant seeds of hope, acceptance, and humanity. Together we stand, divided we fall.

I am being the change I wish to see in the world. What side of history will you be on?

CREATE CHANGE

JULIE: To all my friends from Spring Valley, New York, 10977:

What I've learned is that growing up in Spring Valley gave me the life experience I need to become an informed and active citizen.

I applaud everyone for their efforts these last few weeks to read up on race, racism, anti-racism, etc. Books are wonderful and have a way of helping us connect the dots better.

However, there is no book, documentary, or talk series that can match, articulate, and fully explain the precious life lessons learned from our childhood. I know you know what I'm talking about. I challenge you to think about when you first became aware that there was a thing called race? What did you learn, and how did you learn it?

I challenge you not just to think about it or remember, I want you to reflect. There are no wrong answers here, just your own personal reflection. We learned powerful lessons growing up in Spring Valley. My theory is that we experienced racism, yes, but we also experienced anti-racism *and* at an early age when we weren't even aware of it. That's part of the magic of it. *We do not need to read books to learn how to be an anti-racist.* We have this powerful thing called life experience. Trust in and take action from this place of understanding and you will create change. I promise. xoxo

CLOSING SONG *(optional)*

"Now?" by Stacey Tirro and Hernz Laguerre

End of Play

ABOUT THE AUTHOR

Stacey Tirro is a dance, theatre and physical education teacher at Spring Valley High School in Spring Valley, New York, in the East Ramapo Central School District. Of the 97% of the public-school families who are Black and/or Hispanic, most are first- and/or second-generation immigrants. She has been the advisor for Spring Valley's International Thespian Troupe 721 for 25 years and has produced over 50 plays and musicals with them as well as over 20 concerts with her dance students. Her work has been recognized in *American Theatre Magazine, Theatrefolk, The Unsealed, Strong Women Project Magazine* and *Erika's Lighthouse.* She is proud to have produced *How Do We Feel Right Now?*, her debut playscript with her beloved Thespians. It is her hope that the sentiments expressed in this piece are heard with open ears, so that we may create communities that are safer and more inclusive for every person to live their best life.

Made in the USA
Middletown, DE
10 April 2021